Gossamer

Dr. Lobina Kaniz Kalam, MD

Copyright © 2021 by Dr. Lobina Kaniz Kalam, MD.

All rights reserved. No part of this publication may be reproduced, distributed, or transmitted in any form or by any means, including photocopying, recording, or other electronic or mechanical methods without the prior written permission of the publisher. For permission requests, solicit the publisher via the address below through mail or email with the subject line "Attention: Publication Permission".

This publication contains the opinions and ideas of its author. It is intended to provide helpful and informative material on the subjects addressed in the publication. The author and publisher specifically disclaim all responsibility for any liability, loss, or risk, personal or otherwise, which is incurred as a consequence, directly or indirectly, of the use and application of any of the contents of this book.

Ordering Information:
You may search this book in Amazon, Barnes & Nobles and other online retailers by searching using the ISBN below.

ISBN (eBook):
ISBN (Paperback):

Table of Contents

1 Irrational: 1
2 Savage: 2
3 Manta-ray: 3
4 Resistance: 4
5 Forgotten: 5
6 Poison: 6
7 Dust: 7
8 Adonis: 8
9 Liberty: 9
10 Burbs of Atlanta: 10
11 Chakra: 11
12 Hourglass: 12
13 Honesty: 13
14 Opal: 14
15 Destiny: 15
16 Begotten: 16
17 Hustle: 17
18 Superego: 18
19 Flux: 19
20 Sovereignty: 20
21 Magic: 21
22 Original Sin: 22
23 Fractal in Space: 23
24 Honest to a Fault: 24
25 Passing Time: 25
26 Pandora's Box: 26
27 Deep Prussian Blue: 27
28 Slippery Slope: 28
29 Love IV: 30
30 Frozen: 32

31	Lead Ore:	33
32	Enslavement:	34
33	Motherland:	36
34	Critical mass:	37
35	Mission:	38
36	Sound:	39
37	My Soul's Possessive Mate:	40
38	Dark Angel:	41
39	My Unseen Love:	42
40	The Onyx Prism:	43
41	Silo:	44
42	Cricket:	45
43	Footbridge:	46
44	Nuances: (G)	47
45	June:	48
46	Holy Marriage:	49
47	Distraction:	50
48	Shallow:	51
49	Forgotten Forever:	52
50	Finial:	53
51	Seventy years:	54
52	Soul Friend:	55
53	Melting: a poem	57
54	Epochs:	58
55	Rain Music:	59
56	Gossamer:	60
57	The Sound of Magnetism:	62
58	The Holy Cow:	64
59	Polaris:	66
60	Lunar Eclipse:	67
61	Time and Existence:	69
62	Technology:	70
63	Matador:	72
64	Jester, such a pester:	73
65	Poetic Justice:	76
66	Atlas:	77

67	Eve:	78
68	Ode to Ophelia:	79
69	Pointed Speech:	80
70	Pensive:	81
71	Bubbly:	83
72	Rain Settles:	84
73	Poem 777:	85
74	The Measure of Effort:	86
75	The Scales of Justice:	88
76	Moon:	89
77	Demons:	90
78	Glacial Ice:	91
79	Currents:	92
80	Movement:	93
81	Royalty:	94
82	Shallow:	95
83	Riddle and Rhyme:	96
84	Core Magma:	97
85	Tenses:	98
86	Earth:	99
87	Strange fruit:	100
88	Vatican:	101
89	Chrysanthemum:	102
90	Poverty:	103
91	Napolean:	104
92	Litmus Test:	105
93	Psychosomatic:	106
94	Floating Ribbon:	107
95	Black Hole:	108
96	Blindness:	109
97	Dreams:	110
98	Beautiful:	111

1.
Irrational:

The very base of my neck
Can crack now
Waxed wooden deck
Creaking with every step
Not of the usual sect

There is an Arc of Fire
That must be extinguished daily
It burns and aches inside
At times the burn feels pleasant
The fire tames when I confide

The rational mind
Cannot comprehend
The irrational circumstances
I find myself in
There seems no end in sight

And therein I begin
Each day, smoke and inhale
How unlike my fellow healers?
To hasten along this
Life of suffering

2.

Savage:

A creature in the night
Huntress by sight
I have a soft spot
Like a newborns fontanelle
Leaping over hurdles as a gazelle

I hunt for pleasure
Certain creature comforts
I hunt for my truffle
Each and every day
A feather's subtle ruffle

I like to think of
Myself as Medusa
That I will stone you with my stare
Serpents in my hair
Asteroid muy hermosa

I could just be a savage
One who could ravage your mind
Until you are quite unsound
I could be limitless in my talent
But alas, that would be too unkind

3.

Manta-ray:

I dream my life away every day
And I do not wish to sleep
For too much longer
I am in my mind but not my body
Inhabited by the unseen daily

I have lost my mind I mean
And, I am but a living body
A flicker of light, a gleam
In the innermost eye
A force field, traction beam

Into your soul I dive
From the uppermost cliffs
Delving into the ocean, I glide
A Manta-ray swimming
With guiding tides

4.

Resistance:

My substance is neither rock nor metal
It is cherry red Jello in the middle
Absorbing shock in this kettle
Blow after blow to the gut hollow
I discover my inner mettle

Do you really want me to belittle?
To get in your face
And be really serious?
I know you will whimper.
I know tears might flow

But at the end of it
You will come to know
What you sought
In the first place
No place for fight or resistance

5.
Forgotten:

Forgotten forever
So, I will have children
I will sire, I will carry
My burden and theirs
For joy everlasting

Forgotten forever
So I will just write
Until my fingers bleed
That will be the bloodline
Lineage and heritage

Forgotten forever
So I trudge on
Go on my daily duty
And hope for
The everyday bounty

Forgotten forever
So I try to capture the moment
In sketches and paints
I draw fine and sinuous lines
To enrapture the body divine

I am young but old
I am coward but bold

6.
Poison:

Shooting bullets is not my style
I prefer the quieter poison
With which I beguile
Elixir or potion
Tempting concoction

I will pour it down your throat
While I hold my crown
Swallow it note by note
And do not
Utter a sound

Once you have slept
I will meet with you again
In a different realm
You will be kept
Gleaming as my precious gem

7.

Dust:

That is nothing
That is simply dust
That is everything
I must trust
That is One therein

That is my beginning
Where my ashes lie
In an urn
Turning into a different being
I am molded and soon I will fly

Never to cry
Live with you
At my side
A companion true
To soar and glide

It is my hope and
My desire
That nothing else shall transpire
To cleave me from you
And end this fire

8.

Adonis:

For you I shall wait
A moon or more
For you I shall
Open the door
For you, oh my,
Need I say more?
I smile as if
I had sighted
Adonis
Or did I get shot
Down by Cupid?
You looked and
I blushed unawares
I did think upon it
Quite deeply and sorely
I longed for your
Heightened pulse
Which, how funny,
I did myself measure
And it was certainly
My pleasure

9.

Liberty:

The attainable
And the unattainable
It changes the milieu
The lens
On spectacles

When I think of possibilities
My mind wanders free
Into your arms I fall
Wanting my dream's call
To become my reality

When I am given
My liberty
Set free from my cage
I scan the territory
Step into the forest

I discover
What it is I was searching for
I hear slingshots
Whizzing through
The air and more

I realize a hunter is
Out there in the midst
That is when I leap
Back into my cage
To keep

10.
Burbs of Atlanta:

Lord have mercy,
Where does the time go?
Away it flies to and fro
I recall the
Swamps of Georgia

No I jest
It was just the burbs
Of Atlanta
Holla!
Yell for mo'!

This sure ain't
What my Mama
Told me so
Once when I was younger
And a whole lot stronger

I dreamt of shores yonder
However I could not
Reach the banks
I was pulled back
Yanked

Redirected and shifted
Towards a different location
One that overtook my vocation
Disaster averted
A fatality thwarted

11.
Chakra:

At the base chakra
I dwell in standstill
At head chakra
I fly with a tailspin
At my heart chakra
There is an ache within
At my throat chakra
I breathe you in
At the solar plexus
Chakra zone
My ozone soul resides
In the pelvic chakra
Yin and yang collide

12.

Hourglass:

Half of everything
Is how you look
Into things
Crystal hourglass
Emptying

Grains of sand
Passing through
A rock and a hard place
To find peace
Nadir at the base

From celestial zenith
Down to middle earth
To live and to learn
To conform
And to yearn

Until the point is reached
Thought over and
Almost preached
Soul universal, eternal
Corpus evanescent and ephemeral

13.

Honesty:

To be honest with yourself
What is the meaning of it?
Shall I throw myself
Off the tallest waterfalls
And say that I might die?

Shall I think that all time
Will pass me by?
That one day
As I grow wise
Will regret be my demise?

Wrap its thorned vines
Around my mind?
Choke me and
Leave me there behind
Demented, wound up, unfurled and bound

Shall I tell you the truth?
I know you are not aware.
I know you cannot handle it.
A supernova redshift
Points to my Universe expanding its way

14.

Opal:

You are not mine
You are an
Iridescent Opal
Shining and cut
So fine

Within you
I see flecks
Of molten lava red
Scattered around with
Prussian Blue threads

Encased in
Brilliant gold
I wonder on who's
Hands and fingers
You will adorn

15.

Destiny:

I am flattered that
He is flattered
He is sane
I am clearly insane
Therein lies my answer

Too slowly
Does it sink
Into the brain
Love and desire
What a peculiar fire

I cannot help
The fate I was given
Destiny took me to a place
Quite uncharted
And unproven

I look for my fire
Escape
On the hundredth floor
My abode
Living, dreaming, and more

16.

Begotten:

Men unnerve me
Women anger me
I stay Zen
In a tantric
Kind of way
Inner panic
Melts away
I will not
Meet your eyes
For a second more
You might just
Settle
My score

Time moves so slowly now
Thick, mellow,
Warm and yellow
Honey runs my mind
Saccharine awakening
Innocent forsaking

Beget and begotten
Beholden to your stare
All cares forgotten
Disquiet in my
Quiet existence

17.

Hustle:

It is the hum of car
Machinery
That tilts me toward
A certain misery
I wish it were easier
People near crazed
With fury
Utter stupidity
It infuriates me
How can this be?
Fellow man and
Woman alike
Care for non other
Than their ego's flight
I take in the morning
Sip my caffeine
Clench the Masseter
Muscle
And await the day's
Hustle

18.

Superego:

I will be bound
I allow myself to be tied
And everyday you spied
I was not unaware
But stuporous with every stare

Must be my superego
That stops me in my steps
As I approach you
Stolen keys to my ingress
But alas, I digress

Let me kiss my love
And remind myself
That I am his
I don't know
Quite what this is

This mosquito buzzing
I want to be bit by
It almost reminds me
Of emerald dragonflies

Want him fed with my
Vein's blood by and by
It might be my very
Impatient
Tempestuous soul that
But awaits you.

19.

Flux:

There is too much at flux
There is too much at stake
My innards churn
At every mistake
About to unfurl
I unleash my anger
I cry out for stupor
And await disaster
What the heart wants,
And what it gets?
How curious an effect?
I want warmth and embrace
I long for conversation in grace
What I got I wonder?
If perhaps I ponder
Just a bit longer
Would I discover?
My bliss stated life
This and that sort of
Strife.

20.

Sovereignty:

That's exactly how the water flew
That's exactly when I knew
This life is ephemeral
Passing and lasting
A few days or more
Dying there as I was
Thirsty and weak
I called out for you
How could you?!
My vase with purple orchids
I had given over
Alas, all I got, I suffered
A millennia passes
And how strange?
You remember
My name and my classes
The lessons I had taught you
The care and nurture
Bestowed on you
Now you ask for forgiveness
Will it be my pleasure,
Or my sovereignty
I hand over
I ask only for the explicable
Can you fulfill
What it is I care for?

21.

Magic:

My entire life is some
Illusion
I am but a bit curious
For a solution
Reality obscures vision
Like fog and downpour
High treason in times
Of turmoil
Magic come and goes
Now you see me
Then you won't
As a ghost
I will fade away
Revisit you someday
Dream by day
And toss
The night away
Give me solid
Concrete blocks
To count my fortress
Fortified and exact
Then I shall let you enter
Sit down to dine
Drink my best white wine
Warmth and shelter
I shall provide
And at the least,
I shall be your guide.

22.

Original Sin:

I am possessed by you
You are from the
Other side
This is like
Original Sin

Squeeze my heart
And I will kiss you
Until you die
Pass to the Night side
Uncompromising pull

I say this to myself
As my mind reaches yours
Eyes closed
Breath in sync
Longing for precious more

If you could only see
This play of light
Dance across my chest
Pirouette and leap forward
Step back and admire

23.

Fractal in Space:

Could this point lead elsewhere?
Could this be my fractal
Expressway
To other realms and places?
Can I go unseen?

A smile appears inside
These wormholes in my mind
Dark matter and energy
Abound!
Where can I call home?
Having flown so far
So long?

What is it I seek?
Aware of time
I await my fate
Explorer in this
Fractal of Space

24.

Honest to a Fault:

He he, ha ha!
I am honest
To a Fault
I'll tell you
Truthfully
Always
You may blush
You may withdraw
You may yell
You do not know me
Beware
What I say
To your innermost soul
Your Id, ego, superego
Must decipher
This code
That is how I reach
That is how I speak

25.

Passing Time:

I am filled to the brim
With life
I am being taken care of
I am a being,
Entirely exposed
And I stir inside
Expectantly

My beloved breathes with me
His thoughts fleet with mine
Passing Time
Ruling with light airy notes
Firm and fortified

Dominion far and high
Parallel universe
Passing Time
Scrutinizing eye, mind
Waiting, waiting, waiting
Passing Time

26.

Pandora's Box:

This music that fills my air
Is like wooing a woman
No perturbations right now please
I have sunk into it
Buried underground in light.

My heart soars in flight
Mind reaching higher highs
Drowning in the deepest blue
Sink hole of the sea
Floating around ever-green.

I want to revel in it
Day after day
I have made my discovery
My secret garden,
My Pandora's box
Is ever open.

Whiplash scars on my back
Enduring life's Kung Fu moves
If you only knew
I bathe with the sun
I am but one.

27.

Deep Prussian Blue:

The deepest Prussian Blue anomaly
Much too intense to stand straight
It does take, such skill
Piercing retina, optic nerve, then brain
Stirring the spirit
And then in hot pinks, does it end?

I reached out and,
I pulled out, and,
I strangled it, and,
I conquered it,
My innermost demons,
That is.

Maybe that is the reason
Behind this state
This state of blowing flow
This deep Prussian Blue
Never does let me go

28.

Slippery Slope:

Heavy lidded I wake
To sight you
By my side

I need you for my
Sanity
I am filled up
To the brim

Finally found
The caretaker of
My gardens
Orchids
Fragrant and in
Bloom now

Once I was but
A mound of flesh
Breathing and in pain
Thoughts less than
A twig unable to utter
The slightest word
Yay or nay

I slept like this
For year upon year
Waiting for a hint
Of light
To enter my heart
Awaken my mind

My memory
Ever failing
My breath
Ever gasping
My eyes
Ever wide
Tears in them both
My mouth
Ever so dry

How am I
So different?
That I cannot
Smile.
Cannot feel
Cannot think or
Taste?

Heavy lidded I dream
Of my past and
Then I catch you
Glancing at me.
Such a slippery slope.

29.

Love IV:

Was it when we married?
Did you then look into my eyes?
Did you not know then?
I sat there in my anguish
I could not read
Did you not know then?

This intensity that builds
Inside at the pit
Sweet ripe fruit
That splits at the seams
Aphrodisiac breath
Filling nostrils and eyes

I can almost touch you
Are you there?
Do you know me?
It was I who was waiting
For you to notice
That glimmer in my core

But you did notice
This is why
I am before you
Why did you break it?
Was it just weakness?

I noticed you
But you do not trust
Neither me nor you

It does not matter
You say
Nothing does
So you starve
And breathe
Possessive, obsessive.

30.

Frozen:

My soul had lied
Possibly
When my eyes had met his
Time
Frozen for moments
Perhaps
An hour or more
He entered my mind
He remained there
Probably for eternity
We stood
Unaware of everything
Rain
From Heaven's door
Poured
He touched
My hand
All but once
A sign of friendship
Perhaps he touched
My heart.

31.

Lead Ore:

I am disgusted
This has nothing to do with dirt
Almost beyond comprehension
My destiny on planet Earth
Reality bends, total suspension

Can I even listen to music?
Can I tolerate it now?
The way it moves
My very insides out
I will shut it down

Lie low, hope to unwind
Think for a moment longer
Till my head clears and
I can once again
Even bear to dine

All I have these days
Is perhaps a passing smile
In terms of joy that is
This is heavy as lead ore
This is the child I once bore

32.

Enslavement:

Introspection
Exploration
Interception
Inception
Of a thought

I never knew what
Freedom was
Enslaved from the
Very start
I was choked by the umbilical

Later I was told
To just sit still and
Stop being a child radical
All I wanted was play friends and sunshine
But hush, keep your secrets inside

Blood stain on my underwear
Welcome to womanhood!
When will you be considering
Parenthood?
Shortly after college, I presume

I cried and wanted
To run far away
To escape the utter misery of everyday
To escape my inevitable insanity one day
I wanted to escape so badly back then

I yelled for hiatus
And in four years
Changed my status
I had found a love true.
Don't be ridiculous, you fool!

Yes ma'am, thank you
I needed a reminder
A clear no for an answer
To realize there's no getting away
From this false ivory tower

33.

Motherland:

The shining ore from the
Motherland
That I wear on each hand
Every day until the doomsday end
Is too beautiful for words
Such that I will never part or bend

Still ponds, lily pads, and
Wooden canoes
Jackfruit and Coconut
Lime trees swaying
Among my mother's rose
Bushes blooming

Gram for gram,
Gram for gram,
Ounce for ounce
I am from the milled grain
That sprouted in this
Poor forsaken tropical terrain

34.

Critical mass:

I have let go
Of nearly everything
I do not belong
To my art nor my profession
I do not need anything

This is the very core
The critical mass
The water can buffer no more
The reaction is bound to happen
Energy comes out of every pore

It might as well
Have been chords played
To unlock your secrets
This melody on the violin
Cut open wide and splayed

I wish to be conductor
I cannot tolerate being lower
Bass any longer
I tremble with the treble
Crumble from the stronger tone

35.
Mission:

I do not care
To know more
Who I kill
Or what I
Ask them for
My mission
Is clear
I have my
Badge of
Honor and my
Flag which
I hold dear
I want my
Purple Heart
On my
Coffin dark
I want my
Progeny to
Bear witness
To this contest
I swear.

36.

Sound:

I bury myself in sound
My drums beating in time
My mind once lost
Now found
Words in rhyme
I am meaningless
Without time
I die with the music
I rise with the rays
My life a bit more tragic
Pinned and it always frays
Somehow I stitch
My wounds like magic
I bury myself in the soil
To be one with the worms
And the snails
I bury myself
In sound and tears

37.

My Soul's Possessive Mate:

I, but a woman
Am captured and bound
Fed only with a glance
Light my need
Fire my coal with blue
White and brown hues
Sanguineous Merlot wine
Is my gift
Dine on butter and cream
A firebird am I
Risen from the depths
Of an abysmal core
To touch Heaven's grace
Is what I long for
Possess my soul
And, I will never let you fly
It is my crown, and,
You are my sapphire blue jewel
A diamond in the rough was I
Now polished, cut open,
And brilliantly facetted
Clarity shines from every angle
It is my voice
Which was always my weapon

38.

Dark Angel:

He grazed my cheek
The other day
The caress of light fingers
I will not forget

He toyed with my hair
As he tried to do with my heart
How can I say?

I am not his
Nor is he mine
We are the same kind

As time unwinds
I turn my head right
In Salaam

39.

My Unseen Love:

Do not speak
Under your breath
Do not think
That I do understand
Nothing
Do not hide
Yourself or your eyes

They are what I need most
It is your soul
My food
It is you and your being

Water does not satisfy
Nor does anything

I must sight you
Or, I will fight you
Ignite you
Instill fear in you

Is that not why?

40.
The Onyx Prism:

The Onyx prism eyes
Times cold, slow, tame
Look as if jailed
And charcoal dulled
A glimpse from you
Was all that was needed
Now, the prism catches flame
I cannot look
I must not look,
For shame
My youth gone
In it's place
Nothing, nothing,
But yearning
For your
Embrace

41.

Silo:

The pearls of grain,
Stored for month on end
Wheat bends with the breeze
Trout and potatoes for dinner
The weekly apple pie
Children's mouths to feed
The tractor trailer parks
Pan handling for gold nuggets
A life of quiet stillness and toil
Grandma knits scarves and booties
Grandpa with his pipe and
Suspenders
Bohemian bliss
Their chest of gold
Is the Silo

42.

Cricket:

The violin that they play at dusk
The air scented with musk, incense,
And, Orchids
The hum of Crickets
The Cicadas fanning their wings
Like a finely tuned harp
The Lightening bug
With its helicopter movements
I catch them all
In my palms
They are the orchestra
Of my nightfall
They candlelight
My footsteps

43.

Footbridge:

I crossed a footbridge once
Over Giverny pond
Crossed and gazed
At the floating artwork
I crossed over without a care
I did not once look back
The beauty was everywhere
I looked at the light ahead
I looked at the purple-white
Water lily
And smiled, for,
I realized that
Was once me

44.

Nuances: (G)

Catch the breeze in a nuance,
If you will
Catch the light in a prism
Refraction in the oceans
Catch the nuance of a
Marlin's fins
The nuance of my thoughts
Are harder to catch
Than you think
Time's nuances will
Test you,
I think

45.

June:

I am not June in the Summer
I am the Autumn turning hue
I am colorful as earthenware
Wreaths and Poinsettias in my hair

I am the falling leaves of the Maple tree
I am your reckoning of Winter
Bitter cold

I am not June
I may be Spring with
May Day flowers
I may be your
Awakening from coma

46.

Holy Marriage:

I shall marry
You with twine
I shall marry
You in time
I shall marry
You in rhyme
I shall marry
You with a twig
Offering
I shall marry
You with a leaf
Of any kind
For I am
Yours, and
You are mine

47.

Distraction:

If you continually distract me,
How do you expect me to
Remember the minutia of my day?
My thoughts might fly away
Settle my mind on a few
Things at a time
Linearly,
Not circularity,
With certainty,
I write and think
Constantly
And relax
With musicality
The rhythm in my feet
The drum beats
In thin eardrums
Resonate
Signal my
Metronome pen

48.

Shallow:

There is some symmetry
There is a mark of beauty
Upon your face
Which endures in my mind
Like a symphony for all eternity

I noticed your stance and gait
How you slouch and await
My glance and statements
That is the testament
That there is more to this

Time is the enemy
And my best friend
There is too much conflict within me
To fully comprehend
This Nirvana non-existence

How can I be so shallow?
To be given and
Yet not know?
My muscles tense and relax
Yet I ask for more

I want to pass into oblivion
Prime time now and then
I just cannot justify the end
The meaning of my very being
And why I must not pretend

49.

Forgotten Forever:

Forgotten forever
So, I will have children
I will sire, I will carry
My burden and theirs
For joy everlasting

Forgotten forever
So I will just write
Until my fingers bleed
That will be the bloodline
Lineage and heritage

Forgotten forever
So trudge on
Go on my daily duty
And hope for
The everyday bounty

Forgotten forever
So I try to capture
The moment
In sketches and paints
I draw fine sinusoidal lines
To capture the body divine

I am young but old
I am coward but bold

50.

Finial:

My eyes are everything
I fear if I could not see
What was in front of me
I would fall miserably
I would fracture my mind

Split in half as a melon
Ripe pitted honeydew
Juices seeping
As I weep in darkness
My mind races black and blue

I would come to a halt
Reflect and revolt
I would scream
Mercy me!
Why further torture me?

Would I learn Braille to survive?

Or would I pass
Each day in denial?
Would I finish last?
Or could I discover?

The silvery glass finial
The finish to this endeavor

51.

Seventy years:

I'm leaning on
Seventy years
From now
To meet your eyes
I'm wishing for
That rainbow
Over there
Over the river bend
Over the mountain's
End
Once brown
Meets blue
Hazel arises
Anew
I'm leaning on
That tree trunk
For just a
Few moments
To rest and regain
To catch my breath
From that strain.

52.

Soul Friend:

Soul friend?
Did you recognize me
In Blue?
The Haze,
Surrounding you?
Everything that night
And Day following,
Did I stand out to you?
Ultramarine Blue?
On top
Black heart
And down
You found me there
For a moment,
You called
Me near
We said our
Hellos and
Then goodbyes
We denied
Our Soul's
Bond, not,
For a millennium
We were
Gemini Twins
Encompassed
In Universal spin
Our bellies were

Connected once
Therein
And I am your
Friend and Companion
Ever more and since.

53.

Melting: a poem

Time melts
In despair
Time melts
In highs and lows
Time melts
In discovery
Of a glance
A look inside
A closer insight
Time melts me
I cannot withstand
A test such as this
Forever, ever,
More, and, to
Another realm
Time melts me
Lava molten and
Amber solid
Fossilized interior
To extract and
Breathe once again
This tainted science
Courier to Humanity
Alliance of exteriors
Multiple personalities
Time melts me
Circular, linear, resounding
And, when I place
My lips upon my love,
I will think all time
Has ended ever since.

54.

Epochs:

I am blind in the darkness
Aware of doom
I am deaf in the bombardment
Silencing boom
I am dumb in speech
My cries cannot beseech
There is no one for me here
My mind is dulled
It cannot reach
For a precious memory
Yesterday or in between
The Epochs of my years
I starve. I stare
Into a mirror
And I wonder
How can I get nearer?
What do I see?
It's just a small pool
Of water beside me
That I do not care to Drink.

55.

Rain Music:

Sometimes
The only comfort
I find is in the Rain
The downpour
In sheets
Of music
Written by
One I will not name
What times are these?
When I cannot speak my mind?
When I cannot open
My mouth?
At times,
The only comfort
I find is in the Rain
When the rain
Beats change rhythm
In time,
The metronome moves
In my very insides
My heart drops with
The frequency
My soul soars
With its intensity
Most times,
The only comfort
I find is in
The Rain.

56.

Gossamer:

In my Alcove
On floor numero
Three
A Curtain blew
Across me
A gossamer fabric
While windows
Were closed
Pure Energy
Next to a manicured
Park
With all sorts of trees, shrubs, flowers,
And such
With a bench
Where I once sat
With Angels
And discussed the
Battle ahead
With Demons
Oh, is Not life tenuous?
They had asked,
Gossamer fabric
Blowing in the past?
I stitched one and
Saved nine
I bid adieu
I went on my merry way
On a walk far aways

Gained momentum
Leaped forward Quantum
Light years ahead
Of everyone
Even Aliens.
So Sublime,
They say.

57.

The Sound of Magnetism:

My Soul had lied
Possibly
When my eyes had met his
Time, Frozen for moments
Perhaps
An hour or more
He entered my mind
He remained there
Probably for Eternity
We stood
Unaware of everything
Rain from Heavens door
Poured
He touched my hand
All but once
A sign of friendship
Perhaps he touched
My heart
Indeed my mind
From that moment on
Lingered around his fingers
Langur over his gaze
I could not care
For another soul
After this
My soul had lied
Possibly?
Eyes ablaze

Wife with fear
Pupils coal darkened
Perhaps my soul
Had lied?
It is the sound of
Magnetism
That kept me
Frozen and then
Thawing slowly
Dripping
Perhaps my soul had
Spoken the Truth

58.

The Holy Cow:

The green pastures
Behind my
House, little
On the Prairie
Dandelion greens
As my Salad
With Vinegar dressing
At the least
I have my
Oxen and my
Milk Cow
One to pull the
Weight of the
Autumn Harvest
And the other
To feed my
Ten Children
From Winter's
Starving
As I grow older,
And my children
Get wiser
My oxen tire
And long for
Hours and hours
Of Slumber
I take out my blade and
Make my way

To the Barn
For I know
In my Soul,
This oxen of mine
Deserve more than a
Slow decline
One gash to the
Throat, and
This oxen of
Mine pass
To the Heavenly realm,
I am left with Meat,
Tendons, and Bones
For my wife's
Anniversary Stew
With Barley, carrots,
And Potatoes Blue.

59.

Polaris:

As the rain drops
Pour from the
Heavens
Unto glass
Ceilings
I could not
Break
I saw a
Billion Crown
Formations Synchronized
Dancing, and
Leaping, Twinkling
As the Polaris
Above my
Planet

60.

Lunar Eclipse:

At 3:45 in
The morning
I awoke
The window
Called my name
It spoke
And, I gazed
Upwards
A Halo lining
Around the
Half Moon-Shine
Was it mine?
Was it for this
Very moment in time?
A Voice.
What is your
One wish?
In a flash,
I decided
It was for a
Quick ending
To this life
Never-ending
Striving
Did I get
Some sort of
Accolade?
Applause?

Perhaps one I
Could not hear?
Could not see?
Was that my gift?
For being me?

61.

Time and Existence:

Time sits on a Sturdy Throne
Time is always Blind
Time lends a helping hand
Time with the Eternal
Burning Flame
Time is Fluid Motion
Like Water
You exist in Beauty
And then you
Grow old and Grey
Time awaits you
Time will Test you

62.

Technology:

If you knew who
Zeus was,
You would be scared
He created Mankind
And his woman
Race out of the
Rib on the left
He did it not
Out of love
He did it out
Of Boredom
One could never
Figure Out
Cloak, Uncloak
I am The
Analyst
From Virgo
Quadrant
Sector 7,
Field 3
Station 1.0
Time Earth 2017
Point 7 Zero
How are you?
Oh, I see,
May I get you a
Cup of Coffee?
Have a seat

I will ask you this:
Who do you
Belong to?
A Borg in
The Matrix?
You cannot
Break it!
I Serve The One
Do you want to
Be Released?
Fear, once again,
I See.
Stay where you
Are
I will command thee
Take this Scroll
Do Not Trust
Technology.

63.

Matador:

Divide and conquer,
Conquistador?
A Matador
Am I!
I, with my Eye
Measured his
Movements
He charged
At me fiercely
With a whisk of
My cape, Gilt
Golden Gate
He fell into
A whirlpool
A spell was cast
He knelt at last
He met my eyes
Once more
And rather than
Stab him in the back
I went for the Carotid
As it was Kinder
For his last
Gasp

64.

Jester, such a pester:

Oh! I wish these
Mosquitoes would
Fly away
Leave me alone
And My sweet
Blood Holy
Oh My Lord!
What is this?
A Mark on my
Skin?
Spit on the Devil!
I Say!
SEE, What
Did you say?
Think!
What?
Zombies and
Vampires
Everywhere!
What!?
What did you say?
Fear!
What?
What did you say?
Understand!
What?!
What did you say?
What?!

Demon.
What?!
What did you say?
What?!
What did you
Carry out?
What?!
What did you say?
What!?
What did you Say?
What!?
What did you
SEE?!
What!?
What did you say?
Say What?!!
What!
I was Number 3,
I knew Number 2,
Was Dark Angel
No more
I knew Number 1
Was mine,
I knew
Time.
I knew of
Your foolish
Existence
It was but a matter
Of mathematics
In my Pictorial
Mind
You See,
Zeus calls
Me Hera,
But, Hera is

Not your wife!
I am Not
Aphrodite
For, I do Not
Love you.
I am Pallas
Athena!
I am Wisdom
Better than
Love, at
Times.
I am Christ!
Can you surmise?
I am Number 3,
Archangel
Creation
I am Not God
Everlasting
I cannot
Forgive you
Your Sins
I can only
Laugh at you
Teach you,
For it is only
Time that you
Will Exist.

65.

Poetic Justice:

I might as well
Fly into a Black Hole
And Emerge on the
Other Side
As a Ray of Light
In another Dimension
In Space-Time
I did Not arrive here
To bow down to anyone
I did Not arrive here
To bow down to Shaitan
I came for The Slaughter
I came in the Name of Blood
I came in the Name of
Divine Honor
I came to SEE My
Joy
In your Fear
I arrived right on
Atomic time
To expose
This Negative
Film
Nightmare of
Mine.

66.
Atlas:

Atlas Shrugged
To the right
And to the left
Atlas knelt
To carry the
Weight so heavy
I wonder if
Atlas ever wept?
Ever Slept?
Did Atlas Rise?
Like a Wave's Crest?
Did the Moon lift
His arms up
High towards the Heavens?
Did the Sun Rays
Divulge their secret
To the wave?
Sea Foam Salination
Meets the Trade Winds
Of The Eastern Lands,
And off!
Flies a bubble
Carrying a Seed
An Orb of magic
A wish, a Kiss
For the Soil.

67.

Eve:

Eve, my dear
Did you pluck
Off that stem
Off that branch
Off that tree?
Just to Upset me?
Eve, my dear
Did you think once?
Did you think twice?
Did you think thrice?
Eve, my dear
Did the Apple Sun
Of My eye entice you?
Silence. Too much pain,
I SEE.
Eve, my dear,
You ate of the
Apple in My Garden
As you Loved Adam
And Not Me.

68.

Ode to Ophelia:

I have no one to
Talk to
I have no God
To understand me
I choke with
The pain pent up
Bury myself in blankets
Rest my exhaustion
To rest for
Some time
Until the day
Breaks and
I have to
Face food again
If I close my eyes
Could I taste
The Ambrosia
Of Life?
Could I float
Away in a dreamscape
Where there are
Prairies of Butterflies?

69.

Pointed Speech:

All that I know,
It bore
A fire burning
At the Heart's core
Drilling into a Depth
Fahrenheit 412
Where we slept
Night after night
41 Days until
You woke up
In Fright
Cold sweat
Hairs on edge
You just realized
Who you just met
Pointed Speech
You closed the door
And tried to
Sleep once more
I fumed smoke
My cigar in hand
My Cognac
My Discovery
That very night
Told me exactly
The Scope of
My Sight.

70.

Pensive:

Oh, let me not
Think of the wilted
Roses and Hydrangea
In my Vases
Let me smell them
So as not
To waste their beauty
Let me taste a Petal
For sweetness
Ah, the fragrance
Entered my nostrils
Like a Genie
In a bottle
Once I had
Wished for
A Garden much
Larger than this
I had wished
For an Oasis
In the Saharan
Desert
Where I could
Drink from a
Fountain beneath
A Rock by
The Shaded Palm Tree
A Breeze with a Wisp
Would lift

Every tendril
And unmask me
It's difficult for
Me to breathe
I step aside
I edge myself
Closer to the
Stillness of the
Reflecting Pond
I look inside
Time comes to
A Halt
My vision blurs
My Soul itself stirs
A Dance of Light
In the pit.

71.

Bubbly:

I was quiet
Bubbly, Sweet
Always
Champagne toast
That I knew
A Sip from
From my Glass
Could Certainly
Affect you
That smile crawled
It's way Ever
So Slyly
Unto your face
Wisdom which
Was Ages Old
Stirred Soul
With Grace
Did you know?
The Champagne
Grape was the
Smallest of
Them all?

72.

Rain Settles:

Rain Settles
Everything
May it rain
Everywhere
May it wash
The Atmosphere
May it seep
Into the very
Soul of Gaia
May it Replenish
May it Sprout
Once More
May it Clean
The Ocean layers
May it Monsoon
Over The Deserts

73.

Poem 777:

When I look back,
I SEE, a person who has tested me,
Pushed me to my human limits,
While knowing in his heart of my Kindness.
I will look back and I will
Remember Nothing
Of the Pain and Sorrow
I will go forwards
Into Tomorrow
I knew all along of your sad tale of losses
You confused the masses
I will look back at Yesterday as if it scarred my Back
With lashes of leather whips!
I bled for my Ebony
Keys on my White Piano
I loved and I lost all
That I knew.
The Curse of Iblis
And Lucifer his Gemini
Twin did almost kill me,
I look back, and,
Amnesia takes over me
I look forward to passing
Into Eternity.
I will be with My Maker
As in this Realm and
He has Played
Matchmaker
Quite Well.

74.

The Measure of Effort:

I scan my Eyes
Through Life
They rest on what they spy
A fraction of a second passes by
Before I chew
Like a She-wolf in the Night
I awake by Daylight
I prepare to Hunt
Again for my morning Hunger
I Hunt alone
My pack left me years ago
My Efforts Must be Measured
I cannot be Pressured
To move one way
Or Another
In a Direction Negative
Towards a Black Hole
Where I do Not belong
My Efforts Must be Measured
I cannot Afford to Err
In this Decision
It requires all I have
To give in terms
Of Precision
My Efforts Must be
Measured
I cannot waste my
Energy output

Or resources
In any other way
My Blood Courses
Day After Day.

75.

The Scales of Justice:

The scales of Justice
Are in my hands
Fulcrum is where I stand
A good list on the right
A bad list on the left
The scales shift everyday
In every beating heart
In every way
My septar are flowers
My crown of gold, invisible
Did you forget Moses, Jesus?
Have you lost God?
Where shall you find Him?
Over one hundred thousand have
Come and gone as
Prophets
All were Human
With the range of emotions in their pockets.
Sara was one of them
Were they given drugs
For their message of
Divinity?
How shall you Control
Christ this time?
You shall think twice,
Thrice, sublimely.

76.

Moon:

What is this Cloud
Hiding the moon?
Where is the Wind?
I need it, to push it through
To un-blind my
Sight and move my Blood
Make it course
In my arteries and capillaries
Make it feed my Brain tissue
Make it dilate my pupil
Until the moonlight
Hits my retina and Awakens me more
Alas, I sight the Crescent I was awaiting
This sliver of Silver
I want wrapped
Around my neck
Or on top of my head
As a glowing Halo
I wish to Fly and Soar
Towards that Cloud
That once billowed
That battleship with
Nineteen oars
My heart knows
Nothing more of Time
Except that the Moon
Changes shape
And pushes Tides

77.

Demons:

They will crunch numbers
And justify the means and a disaster
Until, there is some
Normalcy to their
Utter Lunacy
Strengthen my Heart
Father, I pray!
I long, I wish to part
Sooner rather than later
These demons, they sway
Their Sickles made of
Plutonium-like Titanium
These are as the
Sands of the Sea,
A multitude of Grim-Reapers
What they see
Of the Sun?
I often ponder
Hard leaden shells of
Missiles and guns.

78.

Glacial Ice:

Art is for articulation
True inner speculation
Sometimes the smoke
Bothers my eyes
I hate those damn Spies
I turn my wipers on
My headlights on full beam
I wish the fog was gone
So I could see straight
On the path, this dream
I push the gas pedal full on
Head on my own way
In my racing green Jaguar that I got
What a deal!, I say
I put my blue contacts on
To disguise myself
In these dire hours
As a wintry Alaskan Husky
Plowing through snow and glacial ice towers

79.

Currents:

I am one with the Music
I heard it in my back
It's like an abyss inside
Like a free spinning planet
A nudge here and there
That is the crux of
My unhappiness
I might decline
Into some lunacy
I was looking for
Some scraps and shards
Let's see what it is?
Which way the currents push
The Tide.

80.

Movement:

That is the crux
That is the Pinnacle
That is the climax
Of that Mountain
Movement and More
Now the plates
Did Collide
Continents nudged
Sideways and forwards
The Magma oiled it all
I was not informed
But like a psychic
I analyzed it deeply
I concluded my
Own Holy Journey

81.

Royalty:

My Rabbi is kind to me
His smile tells me
That he may know me
How can I express
My hidden identity?
I am just from
The Eastern lands
My skin brown and tanned
Royalty in my
Veins and Arteries
Loyalty to Humanity
Peace emanating
From mine eyes
I shall give you my home,
If you give me my Throne.

82.

Shallow:

There is some symmetry
There is a mark of beauty
Upon your face
Which ensures in my mind
Like a symphony for all eternity
I noticed your stance and gait
How you slouch and await
My glance and statements
That is the Testament
That there is more to this
Time is the enemy
And my best friend
There is too much conflict within me
To fully grasp and comprehend
This Nirvana non-existence
How can I be so shallow?
To be Anointed and yet not know?
My muscles tense and relax to His call
Yet, I ask for more?
I cannot figure out my makeup
Too thick eyeliner or wrong shade of coverup
I want to pass into oblivion
Prime time now and then
I just cannot justify the End
The meaning to my very being
And why I must not Pretend.

83.

Riddle and Rhyme:

This is what happened
A long long time ago
When I spoke
To the Birds in the Tree
And suddenly, they answered me
They spoke in Riddle
They Chirped in Rhyme
They called My name
As if all Time
Had stopped all Shame
Just lie down
Organic Honey,
Stay Quiet, face down
While I whip you
For Just Ten Minutes
Over time and Space
Stay Patient
My Grace Will
Shine on your face
My Son's Torch
After the Race,
Will be your guide
To end this
Path of Blind Torture at
It's own Pace.

84.

Core Magma:

I will send them all
Straight to The Core
Magma
The heart of Planet Earth
To burn at 1.0 Billion
Degrees for about 100
Years or more
That is what is called for
Republicans most of all
That is what it is
It is pure Evil
It is your own handiwork
Of your own witches'
Spindles.

85.

Tenses:

Silver bullet in the night
And, for what reason?
But to change the
Future of all mankind
And end all treason
From birth to present Tense
Forgetting the Trauma
Of Past Tenses
I write my days
Tensed up in my own ways
I spot the fanged
Werewolf creeping
In the darkest hour
He is out for my Blood and Honor
My shield is my Heart,
And My Pen, My Sword

86.

Earth:

Do you see that cloud puffing?
In the sky?
It blew its breath due South
At the trees below
Signaling rain to wash ashore
Then the sun took notice of the wind
And decided to open up its wings
As a Dove does
Or Perhaps Just a Lovebird
Rays penetrated through
To feed that
Spinous Cactus tree
In full bloom
This is termed a
Quantum Leap
Vision Quest
A test
An Ultimatum, at best.

87.

Strange fruit:

Strange Quark
Hanging noosed
I did spy
Star fruit in the very sky
Last night
I sighed
I knew Orion was
Watching over me
As a babe I slept
Ever so softly
In the manger
With the Lamb
And roosters
Kings did visit me
For a moment so briefly
Did they notice my eyes?
Did they look deeply?
I have no hunger for milk
I breathe air slowly
And thus I grow strongly
From my youth
To Adulthood
With my friends
And enemies alike
I preach and pray
For the Right
I look to the left
I stare forward
At the Cross
Strange Starfruit in the Sky.

88.

Vatican:

I look to the sky
Oh Lord!
Give me a sign!
Why must I endure
This garb any longer
I grow weaker, not Stronger.
I look to my people
I see them smile simply
I know they beguile
I pray to God Almighty!
That they survive
This life of strife and struggle
Trials and tribulations
A mountain to Scale
Air thinning
All around
I know Dei
I know Him well
I know His leveling hand
Of Tolerance and Toil
I have seen firsthand and more
In my dreams
I awoke
And was Called upon
I know Time
I know how the mind unwinds.

89.

Chrysanthemum:

Perhaps I should
Try Yoga
To support the
Weight of my head
As it sits on my neck
I need to eat more
Splendidly balanced food
On my tongue
And down the throat
To satiate the stomach core
Does my mother desire
That her life always
Be a blooming flower?
One of her garden's prizes
A Rose for all eyes and contests
Mother dear and friends alike,
The Chrysanthemum
Which blooms is most
Wondrous at night
Black with purple highlights.

90.

Poverty:

Unbelievable,
The way, it Jabs at me
Dagger like in the mix
Mud pie cookie animal snacks
I feed them to my children
And to the ants, my friends
Oh the poverty of reason?!
It is baffling
To say the least
I live to breathe
Each dusty breath as I walk
In the parched
Desert Sun and Sand
How can one not realize it?
Skeleton corpses Beggars on the streets
Where can I turn for a drink?
Of water that will not
Dehydrate me more?

91.

Napolean:

Well, well
My oh my
I did just spy
Napoleon
He has met his
Josephine
And she seems upset
That his ice cream
Was perfectly paved
Smooth in the carton
Oh, how nice!
One man of exacting nature
The other of the loving kind
Napoleon did once conquer
All of France and
Most of Europe
I did not smile
But, a smile did encroach
He was my mentor,
My coach
And I, his secret
Weapon of Choice

92.

Litmus Test:

That is the Litmus test
Can you please press pause,
relax, inhale
And, just process?
My insanity was but an
Act done surreptitiously
But, how can this be?
Slowly the paper test
Strip drenches wet
Rises step by step
In fluid motion
Acid-base commotion
Blue to Crimson
Signaling the release
Of tension
The answer comes through
Clear as night and bright as day
Oxygen transformed
That Hemoglobin
Shape shifted
To carry a burden
Much more
Heavier than that iron ore core
That is my white flag to
Wave.

93.

Psychosomatic:

Psychosomatic
Is it all in my mind?
Am I being called
A lunatic
Am I in a bind
Why can I not heal?
I hurt deeply inside
Death thoughts
Yesterday
And the week
Before
How much more
Can I tolerate?
Mitigate
This situation
Where can I go?
Who can I turn to?
I suppose my only option
Is a serious operation
Where I might not awake
To sleep and not break
Sight that light
At the end of the tunnel
Walk towards it
At the outer limits
Of the funnel.

94.

Floating Ribbon:

Pragmatic
Almost strange
When I am sane
The diagnostics
I discover
You are caustic
Almost insane
Incomprehensible brain
Flying membrane
A floating ribbon
I could almost die
Of shame
Why should I deny?
Trial and tribulation
Atrial fibrillation
A shot to the brain
Oxygen deprivation

95.

Black Hole:

I want to fly
Into a black hole
On the other side
I emerge
Beautiful clouds
As if Heaven
Had touched Earth
I want to dive
Into sound
Light pointing
Towards the sky
I want my soul
Leaping into
Outer space
Into every atomic particle
I am one with the pinnacle
I breathe the air tanks
I give for every meter forward
Into the blackhole
I will not wish for any more

96.

Blindness:

I am blind
By daylight
I cannot make out
Who rules my life
I do not think
Nor perceive
This as devout
I cannot see now
Or in hindsight
I cannot foresee
My life ten years from now
I am running around
Tightly coiled circles
Penitentiary compound
Literally buried
Underground
Questioned until
I am found out
Discovered for what I am
I became sound once again

97.

Dreams:

I could not
Care for anymore
He was indigenous
From that shore
What I felt
Abysmal deep
More
The dream in the
Morning
Escapes me
Quite suddenly
I just smile
Simply
It did not affect me
In the innermost mind
It awaits me
This trance
Spellbound stance
A glance tunneling
Its way into
The heart
And it's Crimson
Blue Dance

98.

Beautiful:

You have made me
Feel beautiful
No need for mirror
I glow outside
At your stare
Into my insides
Perfect sapphire
Gem spinning
Kept me thinking
Of fire
Attire
For your eyes
That admires
You, from
Another dimension
I, still
Earthbound, grounded
Mired in confusion
My life is but
A moment
A glance
As it passes by
A glance
And you stood by me.

www.ingramcontent.com/pod-product-compliance
Lightning Source LLC
Chambersburg PA
CBHW071459070526
44578CB00001B/392